Halfway and Back

Stephen Smithyman

Halfway and Back

For Joy, as always, and for Gerard

Halfway and Back
ISBN 978 1 76109 004 2
Copyright © Stephen Smithyman 2020

First published 2020 by
Ginninderra Press
PO Box 3461 Port Adelaide 5015
www.ginninderrapress.com.au

Contents

At the Memorial to Angus MacMillan	7
Beyond the Maps	8
Driving to the Supermarket	11
Walking With My Dog By the Merri Creek	12
30th Anniversary Poem	14
Birthday Dinner on Brunswick Street	17
Buying a Piano	19
At the Tip	21
Dawn Service	23
The Two-bob Haircut	24
Milford Beach	27
1976	28
Farewell to Kendrick and Mary	29
Last of Summer	30
An Exhibition of Monet	31
Passing in the Void	32
Goldberg Variations	34
Taking a Turn	36
For My Brother, On Reading He Had Bought a Truck	37
Near and Far	38
Midwinter Cold	40
On the Death of Neil Armstrong – 25.8.2012	42
Glimpses: Landscape and History – an Ekphrastic Exercise	44
Journey to the Centre	46
Two Days and Nights at Inverloch	49
Waiting at the Sydenham Rail Crossing	54
Lunch at Noodleland	55
The Last Yard Duty	57
Freedom	58
Mendelssohn Octet	59

'The Seasons' With Vincent Van Gogh, at the NGV	60
Of Hoons and Balloons	62
On Finding a Jehovah's Witness Magazine…	64
Night Piece	65
Halfway and Back	66
Entering the Crematorium	68
Return to Castlemaine	69
Night of the Supermoon	70
Space Station Passing Over Our House in West Preston	71
The Lumber Room	72
Towards Dawn	75
Reasons Not to Leave Home	76
Acknowledgements	78
About the Author	79

At the Memorial to Angus MacMillan

The riverstone marker at the side of the road declares
this was the site of Angus MacMillan's original home.
No mention here of the two hundred or more Gunaikurnai
MacMillan killed, clearing the land. The English class system
was alive and well – MacMillan, a Scottish crofter, got
fifteen thousand acres on this side of the river; his boss,
an English army captain, got fifty thousand on the other.
Still, MacMillan must have been well satisfied. I recognised
the scene in von Guerard's painting, commissioned
while MacMillan was still flush. True, no bulls lock horns
now in the paddock (one brown, one white), the sad band
of Braiakalung, looking on, has been shunted right out
of the picture and the white, timber homestead is long gone,
but Ben Cruachain and Mount Wellington still stand, wearing
their Scottish and English names as emblems of colonial pride.

Beyond the Maps

(1)

Beyond here, the maps are almost bare –
just a few points of interest and less and less
information in between, like a great void
into which we disappear – the edge of nowhere.
Closer, though, it is almost the same. Certainly,
the maps contain information, but what
do they really show? Do they show the way
the land changes every day, with the light
coming over it, at first slowly, then with a blaze
like an explosion, sending long shadows
racing ahead like smoke over the dry grass?
The mountains stand out clean as a picked bone,
while the trees along the creek are covered
by flocks of cockatoos like freshly fallen snow.

(2)

By midday, the mountains themselves have
disappeared in haze, like a blue-black line
of shadow that haunts the edges of our light-filled
summer days. The heat beats down on the paddocks,
which seem to breathe the air back upwards
in a shimmering, pulsating dance. Birds, insects,
cows and humans succumb to its heady trance.
Only the clouds retain their power of movement, passing
in slow procession from one end of the sky to the other,
then on out of sight. Nothing can hold them back,
not even the coming of the night which waits, hidden
in dark pools among the mountains, for sunset's
fiery cue to emerge and spread itself across the plains.

(3)

Then the night, slowly losing the heat of the day
like a fire going out, the coals crumbling in the grate,
the light draining away to a monotone, while cows,
returned from milking, mooch along the fenceline
and all the birds, from the largest, loudest cocky
to the tiniest, twittering wren fold their wings
and settle down to sleep. Darkness floods the land
like a river. A map is one way of knowing a landscape,
a net thrown over the ground, imaginary lines of control,
but reality has a way of sneaking around the edges,
escaping through the holes. There is, simply, so much
we do not know. That takes time: the slow generations,
crossing and re-crossing the land, learning every bump
and hollow, every dry gully and watering hole,
because their lives depended on it – not a quick glimpse,
like tourists passing through, but a landscape truly
lived in, day by day. And then, as those mountains,
now lost in night, remind us, the greater unknown,
waiting for us somewhere unmapped, out there in the dark.

Driving to the Supermarket

(Rainbow over Preston)

Driving to the supermarket through drizzling rain,
under a leaden sky, bordered by patches
of brilliant sunlight, I stopped at the traffic lights
and looked up, amazed – along with
everyone else – at the most perfect rainbow any
of us had ever seen, arching over Preston,
like some long forgotten promise of God's will.
Each band of colour was absolutely clear
and extraordinarily intense, the condensed essence
of colour, from which all other colours
are born. Signs and wonders…in the parking lot,
people got out of their cars, phones in hand,
to capture the perfect beauty that was fading fast
before their eyes. How could such beauty
vanish so easily? And what about the promise
that seemed to be contained in its perfection –
forgiveness, reconciliation, beginning a new life?
From midwinter dark and cold, everyone's
heart lightened, looking up at that rainbow, which
dazzled momentarily, before merging back to grey.

Walking With My Dog By the Merri Creek

Always, in my mind, I am walking
with my dog by the Merri Creek,
through the Andy Capp Reserve,
across the shaky suspension bridge

and upstream to the Kodak factory,
or downstream, across the busy avenue,
skirting the bottom of the golf course,
and on into Northcote and North Fitzroy.

Always, she glides ahead like an elusive
black shadow, dodging cyclists, dive-
bombed by magpies, stopping only
to play, sniff other dogs and piss on posts.

This is the same park where I walked
with my wife and children, when
the children were very small, in pusher,
on stumbling foot or wobbling bike.

Now the dog is dead, the children
are grown up, my wife and I live
somewhere else, but the Merri Creek
still runs under roads and bridges,

between banks covered by tea-tree
and willows, the debris of last year's floods
caught in their branches, unruly relations
to more recent, planned plantings of eucalypts.

The past is a shadow that flickers
across the mind like a black dog, running
along a path beside the Merri Creek, now
in full sight, now hidden from view,

but always coming back, whether I call
or not. I know now it will never leave me,
anymore than that creek will, tracing
its slow descent from first rise to the sea.

30th Anniversary Poem

1 The Challenge

'Oh God!' you said, 'It's our thirtieth anniversary.'
'Oh God!' I said, 'So it is.' We had both forgotten,
eyeing the steadily increasing New Year's rain (once
I would have regarded that as a portent, a promise
of new life – now I know everything stays pretty much
the same). So I went out and bought a bottle of cheap
Spanish bubbles (something to do with the sunshine?)
and, together, we sat down in front of the TV…
Thirty years ago, we carried my belongings, stuffed
in plastic bags, from my place to yours along suburban
Brunswick Street, at midnight, New Year's Eve, while
rockets exploded, car horns honked, and boats' sirens
moaned out on the harbour. Far and near, drunken
revellers called out 'Happy New Year! Happy New Year!'
to all and sundry, and it seemed, for a little while,
at least, everything was possible… Thirty years later
we have a house that is too big without the children, time
for ourselves, finally, if we can recognise ourselves again,
bubbles, TV and the challenge of that New Year's rain…

II One Lifetime

The sand runs through the hourglass –
the balance tips in the other direction…
our children take us to the Mussel Festival
to celebrate our anniversary. We eat
mussels Thai-style, mussels French-style,
mussels Spanish-style, mussels pickled
'with a hint of truffles', and drink cold beer,
locally brewed. We inspect a vintage car
exhibition – twenty or thirty Morris Minors
all in a row – such inexpressible cuteness!
I remember when people drove cars like that
for real. In the heat of the afternoon, we retire
to the beach below – a narrow strip of sand,
backed by low scrub, pine trees and a reserve,
filled with blaring fairground rides, specially
for the occasion. The beach borders a blue-green sea
so clear and still, it could easily be mistaken
for a lake, were it not for the jet-skis, buzzing
up and down like mosquitoes in the mid-distance,
while, further out, a sailing barque, dressed up
like an old pirate ship, ferries tourists round the bay…
We read, swim, lie out in the sun, burn slightly,
let the day slip by. Perhaps it isn't perfect, but
was it ever meant to be? Still, it's close, as close
as one could wish to come in this lifetime, anyway.

III Sydney For a Day

We fly to Sydney for the day. We see
an exhibition of American painting –
the movement from the periphery
to the centre – and Yoko Ono at the MCA.
We quarrel in an installation, *Before
and After Peace*, and come back together
in a plexiglass labyrinth. Yoko's phone,
at the centre, doesn't answer. Clearly,
we're still on the periphery. Outside,
ten storeys high, a cruise ship lies at anchor,
big as several city blocks. We briefly explore
The Rocks – such poverty and affluence
side by side! – and all presided over
by 'seventies Brutalist commission flats
where people live inside dark, concrete cavities
like Stone Age refugees in caves. Sadly,
we don't have time to ponder these
(or any other) paradoxes as we race
for the train, the airport and the plane.
Our time in Sydney is over and we must run
back to the comforting familiarity of life
in the city we call our own. But not before
we raise a glass of real (though cheap)
French champagne to thirty years together
and the chance – if only! – to do it all again.

Birthday Dinner on Brunswick Street

We park in a derelict building just around the corner
from fashionably grungy Brunswick Street and trudge
across the concrete floor of the roofless, graffitied shell
in pouring rain. We buy beer and bubbles at a nearby
bottleshop and enter the restaurant, surprisingly full
and cheery for a wet Monday night. After a couple
of entrees and a few drinks, I feel the familiar, warm slide
into drunkenness begin. This is Dad as 'sacred monster' –
talking and laughing much too loud, telling 'off' stories
and eating enormously. My wife, beside me, shrinks back
into her own delicious plate of food without a word.
She has no wish to compete in the performance stakes,
but the children and I jostle each other for attention.
I feel the pressure of age – the young want their time
in the sun, now they are finally establishing themselves
in life, while their elders wither and fade. It's only natural,
like flowers in a garden, but it makes me feel ashamed
of my inability to drop my clown prince role, to stop
hogging centre stage. My daughter wants to argue with me,
disputing the sources of my knowledge, not to mention
my spurious, so-called authority, and my son, whose
birthday this is, eats, drinks and argues with both of us,
enthusiastically – which is surely the main point, anyway.
We re-emerge into the rain-slicked, light-refracting tunnel
of Brunswick Street, saying what a happy time it's been
and how we must all do this again soon. And it's true,
as families go, we have the very good luck to be able to say
we're still together, after all this time, we love each other,

we enjoy each other's company, even with all our differences, difficulties, individual successes and failures, separate joys and sadnesses…on a wet, cold night on Brunswick Street, we're able to conclude this hasn't been an idle dream.

Buying a Piano

for Joy

All things wear out with time…and so it is, unfortunately,
with your mother's piano, which has stood, or leant,
against our living room wall for many years.
Back wheels removed, stained and chipped, it is not
the most glamorous of objects, but it has still brought forth,
under your fingertips, visions of beauty, hopes
for a better life, where love and truth are honoured –
the whole, sweet dream of the human heart, expressed
in melody and harmony – or would do, if it were
in better nick, with no bum notes, no sticky keys. Finally,
it has to go. We drive to the piano shop on Bell Street
(that frenzied conduit of cars, trucks and buses, six
packed lanes of traffic, non-stop uproar night and day).
Entering the shop, we are greeted by a baby grand, playing
mysteriously, all by itself – keys going up and down
under invisible hands, drawing out an unwritten tune,
like a scene in a horror movie. We are served by a tall,
silver-bearded, lugubrious-voiced man who emerges
from the back like Dracula, played by Christopher Lee.
He sits at a digital keyboard and riffles through musical phrases –
classical, jazz, rock 'n' roll, harpsichord, organ, Hammond organ,
strings, a whole symphony orchestra – such astonishing skill!
Flowers of music blossom under his fingertips, expand
like clouds, then float away down Bell Street, soothing
the savage beast. We stand before him, mute with wonder,
then dumbly signify this is the one we want. In the office,
we sign the contract with shaking hands and sit back,
scarcely able to believe this new view of ourselves.

We have bought houses and cars, have brought children into this world, but never expected to find ourselves proud possessors of a brand new piano. It waits for us, somewhere out in the shadowy storeroom, all polished ebony and brass, with its silent, as yet unplayed keys, like a promise, like a prayer, in its cardboard coffin box.

At the Tip

The proverbial certainly does not apply here –
this is a veritable cathedral of waste,
dedicated to everything we want to reject,
eliminate, remove from our lives,
a comprehensive purging, complete evacuation.
Life is a process, turning whatever
we once thought was good into rubbish, to be
evaluated by the mysterious guardian
of the gate, who puts his own price on everything.
So, a trailer load of household rubbish
one day costs something and, another, something
quite different, for no discernible reason –
a bit like our famously variable Melbourne weather.
Having passed the guardian at the gate
and suffered God knows what imposition, we follow
the line, white, yellow or blue, that leads
to the particular chapel of disposal we worship at
today. This is where we genuflect, this is
where we kneel, this is where we pray to the ideal
which everywhere consumes us –
to be rid of our waste, to be cleansed, to be free.
But first, we have to back the trailer in.
That ritual humiliation completed (usually with
the grudging assistance of the tip attendant),
we step out of the car, let the tailgate down and begin
to empty the trailer…metals in the metal bin,
timber in the timber bin…all other waste over the edge,
into oblivion. Because that is what we seek,
at the end of this process – sweet oblivion, quietness
and peace, the emptiness of death itself –

or am I reading too much into this situation? However
that may be, I'm satisfied; lunch beckons, a beer,
perhaps an afternoon sleep, after a quick trip to the tip shop
to see what dusty, rusted bargains it may hold…

Dawn Service

Dawn is the time of death, the presenter's portentous voice
informs us, as we wait in the dark, a huge crowd,
with an atmosphere more like a rock concert or a football match
than a memorial service. Even surrounded by that crowd,
we can imagine something of what those men might have felt,
as they waited in their boats to set out for the beach
at Anzac Cove, each isolated by the thought of his imminent death,
a target for Turkish riflemen on the ridges above.
                                                         I, too,
am left alone with my memories – my grandfather,
buried alive on the Western Front, my father's surreal war,
preparing to defend New Zealand with wooden rifles
and imaginary trucks, my own opposition to the Vietnam War,
registering CO and praying my number wouldn't come up…
Somehow we survived these and other vagaries of our lives,
as did the veterans gathered here. Not so the dead.
The band plays 'Abide With Me'. A crackle of gunfire suddenly
makes everything terrifyingly real, as dawn begins
to lighten the sky over the shrine. It is time to make peace
with the dead soldiers, the wrong wars, subsumed
into a larger sadness, the entirely regrettable cost of some kind
of freedom, or, at least, a recognition of what they gave –
the dead soldiers and the walking wounded – however duped,
deluded and misled by cynical politicians they may have been.
Easy to judge; less easy to be judged.
                                      The boats grind ashore
at Anzac Cove in a dark dream of bullets and blood; the service
ends with anthems and entertainment for the whole family.
The crowd breaks up, feeling safer in morning light, surrounded
by the buzz of traffic and the clanking of St Kilda Road trams –
the familiar, comforting sounds of the city waking up to another day.

The Two-bob Haircut

'Mum says cut it short at the sides,
but please leave it long on top.'
That's what I said when I climbed up
onto the board the barber laid
across the arms of the chrome
and leather barber's chair, clutching
the two-shilling coin Mum had given me
firmly in the palm of one sweaty hand.

I was eight or nine years old
and far too young to know much
of the world beyond the confines
of the tiny seaside town where I grew up.
It was enough Mum trusted me
to go to the barber's on my own –
an alarming and enticing place,
vaguely redolent of sin, with
its calendar shots of girls on the wall
and piles of ever so slightly racy magazines.

Not that I really looked at them.
What I loved were the comics.
My brothers and I were not allowed
comics at home. Mother and father
had determined they were not good
for our intellectual development.
They were a furtive pleasure,
to be sampled sitting in the vinyl chairs
along the side wall of the barber's shop,

opposite the mirrors, hoping to delay
the inevitable as long as possible,
that moment when the barber would turn
and say 'Next!', knowing it was me.

I loved Mickey Mouse, Donald Duck,
Green Lantern, the Phantom, Batman –
but most of all I loved Superman,
who flew around in colours
vaguely resembling the American flag,
saving the world. That's who
I wanted to be, handsome, muscular,
admired, not the Clark Kent I already knew
myself to be, with or without glasses.

And so I sat and dreamed,
while the barber (lighting
another cigarette and putting it down
in the ashtray on the counter)
cut, clipped and shaved the sides
of my head, taking care
not to nick my protuberant,
most unSuperman-like ears,
then oiled and combed the hair
on top of my head, so it set
like concrete, which I patted,
wonderingly, all the way home.

I was eight or nine and innocent
of the ways of the world.
I had no idea there could be
falsehood or suffering
on a grand scale, that somewhere,
over seas and through jungles,
there was a place called Vietnam,
where battles were already
being fought and lines being drawn
which would one day blow
this quiet, complacent world apart.

All that was in the future;
I still had my dreams
and my sly, unapproved discoveries –
the rest of my childish growing up to do.
I climbed down from the board,
handed the barber the silver florin
entrusted to my overheated care
(it left a dark mark – of betrayal? –
in the centre of my palm) and walked
out of the barber's shop into
a sleepy street which was slowly waking up.

Milford Beach

At twelve years old, escaping from my parents' perpetual war,
I used to ride my bike, flat out – legs pumping, heart thumping
(I was winning the Tour de France) – along the main road,
past the primary school I had left, at the end of the previous year,
around a roundabout and up the main street of the small, seaside town
where I grew up. Turning off the main street, I followed another
long, straight road past the fish 'n' chip shop and the Picturedrome,
scene of many delirious Saturday afternoon matinees with the local kids,
Jaffas rolling down the aisles, feet drumming on the floor, as the cavalry
came over the hill (shortly after, it became the 'Surfside Ballroom'
in the new 'beat' era that was already dawning), to the beach.
There, I dropped my bike, vaulting from the saddle, cowboy-style,
as the front tyre bit into the sand that crept up the boat ramp between
granite seawalls, built to protect the houses against encroachments
of the stormy sea, and stepped out on the beach. This was my domain,
the kingdom of my childhood, safe and away from home.

As I stood there,
breathing in the salty air that cleared my head and stopped my chest
from heaving, I looked out on that sea, placid and contented, not
wind-whipped and angry, as I knew it could sometimes be. I knew
all its faces and phases, low tide and high; its colours, green, blue,
grey and sandy brown; its moods, so quiet and still, its wavelets
barely turned over, running up the sand, or so wild, its waves reared up
above the seawall, before crashing down, sending ribbons of spume
and clouds of spray flying across the land. I knew all this, yet I
could not believe it would be that way in my own life, that nothing
would ever stay the same, no matter how much I wanted it to (something
I would have to acknowledge, as I came of age), like those restless waters,
running around the world – in that constant movement, a ceaseless change.

1976

That summer, we city boys, eager to try some country life,
rented a small, fibro cottage – a bach, as they called it,
in New Zealand, in those days – beside a tidal inlet,
with mud and mangroves, and a bush covered point
where the local potter lived in splendid isolation.
At high tide, nurses would bring patients from the Home
for Chronic Alcoholics, further along the inlet, down
to the beach across the road for a swim. The only people
more stoned than ourselves, the alcoholics would stand
in the water and let the waves smack them right in the face,
without any reaction. At low tide, one day, a girl came
to our door with an urgent plea for help. She had been riding
her horse across the mudflat and it had got bogged
a long way out, halfway to the other side. We took a spade,
rope and boards – anything we thought might be useful,
in our befuddled state – and set off across the mudflat,
anxiously eyeing the incoming tide. When we got there,
the horse was bogged to its shoulders. We dug around it,
pulled from the front, pushed from the rear, all the time
mindful of that tide, creeping ever closer. We put the boards down,
gradually got it moving, until, eventually, it struggled out –
forequarters clawing first, hindquarters sucking after –
and stood, if not on firm, at least on firmer ground, mud-covered,
flanks heaving, foaming at the nostrils, wild-eyed, terrified, free.

Farewell to Kendrick and Mary

In that photo, then, they sit or lie
by the side of the road, together
and apart, exhausted by their years
of conflict, the love they could not express,

the hate they could not resolve.
Kendrick sits forward, darkly tense,
cradling his camera, on the lookout for birds,
always hoping for that field guide entry.

Mary lies back, warming her poor,
crippled body in the late afternoon
sun, enjoying the momentary respite
from chronic arthritic pain. They do not speak;

they do not need to speak. If they spoke,
what would they say to each other?
Only the usual litany of complaint,
recrimination and abuse, mixed

with the odd, unguarded tenderness
that puzzled others and so prolonged
their 'Dance of Death'. Leave them alone,
memory, let them enjoy this brief

moment of peace, of rest on the journey!
We cannot call them back, reconcile them,
make a blessing out of a curse. They were
mother and father, for better and for worse.

Last of Summer

Squeezing the last drops out of summer,
I mow the lawn, rearrange the garden furniture
and snooze briefly on a sun recliner, sinking into
that contented torpor which is now mostly
childhood memory or overburdened adult's dream.
And dream I do, sweating in the unexpected heat
that soaks into my bones like water from
a warm bath, dissolving the weary flesh until
I'm ten again, lying on the beach, surrendering
to the sounds of waves breaking and gulls
calling overhead, the red behind my eyelids…
There was no end to it, because I knew
of no alternatives – there was no other life. Now,
at sixty-three, I have lived too many different lives
to ever settle comfortably into one again.
So I linger long as I can, without feeling guilty,
without feeling called to the myriad other things
I could be doing with my precious time…
now there's a theme – eh, dear reader?
I could go on, but know I can't. I don't have
the luxury of all that time any more. Wisdom
discovered too little and too late, but still
I determinedly squeeze those last drops of enjoyment
out of the passing season, like juice from a plump,
ripe orange, quenching the parched throat.
I wake with a start, rise stiffly from the recliner,
resuming my normal flesh, go inside and have a beer.

An Exhibition of Monet

To step into that room
was to be suddenly immersed in water –
such calm depths – layer on layer,
of lilies, floating like islands
across the cool, dark pond,
of clouds and trees reflected on
the glassy surface,
height layered on depth,
opaqueness on transparency,
until the head spun
and one lost one's sense of gravity,
swaying free like the stems of lilies,
swimming slowly upwards,
or the branches of willows,
dangling gently down.

The invitation was to spend the afternoon
in contemplation of stillness and fleeting motion,
physical presence and insubstantiality,
only to walk into the next room
and see it all dissolve in fire –
the Japanese bridge and the rose alley
burning red, twisting, collapsing,
the paint slathered on the canvas
to a point almost beyond recognition –

the unforgiving rage and pain of old age.

Passing in the Void

'You reach a stage
where everyone around you dies
and you are left
on the other side, alone.'
So my octogenarian uncle
to my younger brother,
reported to me on the phone
from New Zealand.

At nearly ninety,
my uncle drives
the length of the North Island
and crosses Cook Strait
to visit our aunt –
his older sister –
her sharp mind
slipping into the dullness of senility
in her Nelson nursing home.

So my brother,
longtime nurse in Intensive Care,
sits with a friend of our parents
and holds her hand,
as she lies dying.
One night, she rises up from her bed
and hugs him,
clings to him, he says,
with surprising power and persistence –
'She would not let me go.'
He goes home;
a few hours later, she dies.

The meaning of this?
There is none, except perhaps,
the meeting of two souls,
two minds, two lives
passing in the void,
momentarily recognising each other
before the unending silence,
the everlasting absence,
which is our common destiny.

Goldberg Variations

A rainy night in Melbourne. Together with my wife
and my brother – whom I haven't seen for several years
and may not see for several years again – I catch the train
into the city. We drink beer at a rooftop bar, watch
drifts of mist alternately obscure and reveal the tops
of office blocks, eat Malaysian hawker food in Chinatown,
then run all the way to Southbank to see a woman
play Bach's *Goldberg Variations* (that well-known
cure for insomnia) on the harpsichord. At first,
we can't find the venue. We race past crowded shops
and restaurants, feeling the pressure of time – why
is there always less of it than we think? We attempt
to follow a touch-screen map, which only leads us
deeper into the labyrinth, end up asking the doorman
of a swanky hotel for help and finally find the church,
nestled like a mushroom at the foot of tall trees
in the high-rise forest that is Southbank. Arriving
in a damp, sweaty fluster, we're much relieved
the music hasn't started yet. Instead, the performer
is talking about 'counting variations' (is this
some kind of code?). We settle down, embarrassed,
in the back row of the small, ageing audience –
older even than ourselves, it seems – to listen
to her talk. And so, eventually, to the music,
which is complicated, exuberant, argumentative,
or radiantly simple and tender as a man's conversation
with his God, his wife or his child should be
(or maybe it's just an exercise, an arrangement
of notes for practising skills), while warily eyeing

the enormous wooden cross, suspended like
the sword of Damocles, high on the whitewashed wall
above the ornately painted harpsichord. How we wish
we could believe with Bach, but find ourselves
completely unable to, unless the justification for such belief
can be detected in the most familiar, everyday things –
God revealed in His commonest creation, as it were.
When it's all over, when the last note has faded into silence,
along with the last, warmly appreciative handclap
(there are no encores – as the famous pianist
my wife and I once saw, said 'After that, you want more?'),
the three of us are returned to the rain, the night, the darkness
of our usual confusion, but somehow cleansed, renewed.

Taking a Turn

Brother, I think of you, lying down on a cold floor
in the early hours of the morning because
you 'felt so awful', and I think of our father,
as I have no doubt you did, on the last,
lonely night of his life…let's hope the end
came quickly, mercifully, for him! I think of all of us,
entering late middle-age (or is it early old age?) –
the querulous uncertainty of our lives,
the treacherous turning of our bodies against us.
I feel, no doubt, what you felt when you heard
I had cancer. Any incursion against the family flesh
is experienced as profound disturbance –
we're both under threat here. So I think of you,
as I wake in the early morning hours, first
to pee, then to write this down, to extend to you
the little that I can – my concern, my sympathy,
my hopes for your recovery, my shock at thinking
what you must have gone through, as you lay there,
facing the awful possibility, if it came to that,
of following our father, beyond companionship,
beyond sharing, beyond love, into that final solitude.

For My Brother, On Reading He Had Bought a Truck

Brother, when I read you had bought a truck, the first
in our family – at sixty-plus – my heart lifted within me.
I was reminded of our childhood, digging roads, tunnels
and houses out of the soft, dark earth of the creek bank
at the bottom of the garden. Such massive earthworks,
such massive excavations, waiting to be carted away,
so we could drive our Dinky toys around the town
we were constructing! Now, it seems, you have a truck
of your own to do that with. I am all envy, as I am
of your dream of a 'ten-foot tinny' on the back, suddenly
within your grasp – once, also, a dream of mine, never
to be realised now, I fear. You write further of puttering
out into the bay at evening to set a net for kahawai, to be
hauled in next morning, teeming, you hope, with fish.
I feel the chill in the air, share the excitement of the catch,
the keen anticipation of breakfast in the pan, see
the beauty of the sun, rising over calm, morning water…
ah, brother, I will join you once again in that dawning!

Near and Far

Those memories that stay with us
over a lifetime – the blue egg shape
where the top of my head had been,
as the brown creek water
closed over me for what I knew
was the last time, at the age of six…
or fishtailing wildly up a concealed
gravel side road after the car in which
I was hitchhiking failed to make
a sudden, unannounced right-angle bend
at the end of a long straight, at sixteen
years of age…or sitting in a car,
at twenty-six, with friends, staring
in stunned surprise as another car
came scything up a country road towards us,
completely out of control. With no escape
forward or back, we could only sit
and contemplate our fate. In the end,
the car described a perfect triangle around us –
nose, body and tail – before waltzing away
behind us to become the following car's
concern, running off the road harmlessly,
while we drove on, silent, numb…
or sitting, silent, numb again, at sixty,
with other patients in the cancer ward
of the local hospital, waiting to be called
for my radiation therapy, all of us knowing
some would survive and some would die,
in nature's casual, careless lottery –

those moments when our lives seem
as fragile and exposed as a spider's web,
suspended between two trembling branches,
a fine filigree, which could simply snap off
and blow away in any passing breeze.
They propel us into a life more intensely savoured,
more gratefully appreciated than before,
after acquaintance with that thin wall
which divides the light of our living
from the darkness which waits for us all.

Midwinter Cold

Midwinter in Melbourne chills to the bone. I lie in bed,
coughing, sneezing, blowing my nose and stuffing
soggy tissues in a plastic bag, suspended from the top knob
of my bedside chest of drawers. The bag hangs
ominously open, threatening to spill its noxious contents
across the floor. Like my cold, it must be contained,
controlled. Lying there, cut off from the world, with only
the dog for company, I'm moved to reflect on
how the body can become a prison, when it's no longer free,
when it's given over to illness or injury, so its will
is no longer its own. I think of that phrase, much loved
by my brother – 'The gross body's treason'…
Shakespeare was right: the body is a state and our minds
are the government, but something works
within our bodies to betray us with their very grossness,
their solidity, as opposed to the mind's intangibility,
its capacity to conceive of abstract perfection, unassailable purity.
Trapped by this paradox, we struggle, we suffer.
So, my brother, waking in the night to heed the call of nature,
collapses by his bedroom door, his poor heart racing,
his body rebelling against the mind's authority, its desperate efforts
to assert control, restore order. So, I, recovered a little,
venture out to take a friend, suffering from the same cold,
who has collapsed twice in one day, to Emergency
at his local hospital. Driving towards Carlton, the downtown towers,
wavering in the mist, seem as insubstantial to our grasp
as life itself. I brave the lunchtime traffic, crossing Royal Parade,

to drop him off at the Emergency entrance, an open mouth
which swallows him in to whatever interminable, alarming process
waits for him inside. But sometimes the mind can be
a prison, too. I think of my mother, at the end of her days, driven
half-crazy by strong medication and never-ending pain –
not to mention the sadness of a bad marriage – raging against
her condition, beating the arms of her medical chair,
asking, again and again, the one question we can never answer
'Why am I like this? Why am I like this?' Prison
of the body, prison of the mind – which is worse? We cannot say.
One thing we can say, however. We're all prisoners
of this winter in Melbourne. It holds us in its grip, the one certainty
in a host of uncertainties. Will it never end?
Of course, it will – hard as that may be to believe in the midst
of this cold and early dark, overshadowing the afternoon.
Looking out my window, I see daffodils and jonquils, waving
their fragile heads in a freezing breeze, by the front fence.
We're like those bulbs my wife planted – they wait a long time
in the dank earth before pushing up their shoots,
seeking light, presaging warmth, which they will help us find.

On the Death of Neil Armstrong – 25.8.2012

Can it really be forty-three years
since Neil Armstrong took his first,
tiny step onto the moon and the whole world –
the whole universe – changed? Romance
did not end, as was widely predicted,
but suddenly we were no longer
limited to Mother Earth. For the first time
in our history, we were officially licensed
to leave home.
                    Dear Neil, how bold he was
to take that first step, and how humble since –
scarcely heard of by those of us
who did not closely follow his story!
We were too engrossed in stories
of our own and yet we all remember
that day, that afternoon – where were you?
Like playing cricket when Kennedy died,
or directing a high school play
when Lady Di met her brutal end
against the wall of a Paris tunnel…

I recall that long-distant afternoon,
in a student lounge in New Zealand,
affecting indifference to the flickering images
on the TV screen, forming and dissolving,
in and out of champagne-like bubbles –
a news broadcast from the depths of space! –

with those American voices, droning on
in their space-pro lingo, 'The Eagle has landed!'
I barely knew whether to laugh or cry.
Then the silver-suited hero, stepping out
between the bubbles, descending the little ladder
into the harsh glare of the lunar day and stamping
his tiny imprint on the grey lunar dust…

Did that imprint last forever, together
with the shiny, metallic-looking flag, flexing
on its pole like a theatre thunder sheet,
or did it blow away – sooner rather than later –
hurled into the infinite by the howling solar wind?
And what became of Neil, the humble hero
we had all forgotten about until this day?
Was it enough for him, simply to have been there,
where no man had ever trod (and no woman,
either), so that he did not need our everlasting
love and admiration to follow him into
the shyness and anonymity of the rest of his life?

The story ends, the hero fades away…
bring up the music, roll the credits…yet
something remains of the small man who took
that giant step on behalf of us all and moved
outside his normal realm, the earth, hanging
like a blue, green and white ball below him, against
the blackness of space, punctuated by fiery stars,
into some inconceivable future only he could see.

Glimpses: Landscape and History – an Ekphrastic Exercise

1 *Drying Wildflowers*
(Dame Emily Kngwarreye, 1990)

Drying wildflowers will not die.
Like stars in the sky, they live forever.
Not so with our little lives. We come up,
we are cut down, apparently, in just
one day. Everything changes, nothing
remains the same. The wildflowers smile.
They nod their heads together, dancing
in the wind, drying all the time. They will
outlive us; they outlive nature. In the end,
stars and suns bloom around them. They rise
like balloons to take their true place in the sky.

2 *Portrait of a Woman*
(Russell Drysdale, 1945)

She sits on a wooden bench in front
of a corrugated iron wall, like a theatre curtain,
drawn to reveal the scene – red dirt desert,
the colour of dried blood, and an ominous,
black thundercloud. A parody of Gainsborough,
Reynolds or van Dyck, her fresh, bland face
and thick farm wife's body show pride of possession
over the barren, ancient land. She does not yet know
what she has inherited – the struggle, the guilt,
the aching dryness relieved only by savage downpour
and raging flood. No wildflowers bloom here. The storm
of history gathers over her innocent, young shoulder.

3 *Ghost Gums*
(Albert Namatjira, c. 1952)

From the high ridge with the ghost gums,
on the one side, to the wall of mountains
on the other, the valley is a vision of peace.
Painted in the white man's language, with
a black man's knowledge, this is a place
of quiet contentment and plenty. Even the heat
seems amiable, if intense. The hard leaves
of the gum trees are softened by affection,
as are the twisted shapes of the tree trunks,
climbing the ridge or dotting the valley floor.
Any harshness, familiar to white people, is denied,
except a lingering sadness; ghosts inhabit the land.

4 *Karntakurlanga Jukurrpa*
(Dorothy Napangardi, 2005)

Abstract as concept, abstract as idea,
like words in a foreign language,
densely resistant, requiring effort of will
to understand, they most resemble seed pods
after bushfire, burnt and blackened,
but resilient...hundreds and hundreds of them,
opening to meet their moment of release,
the seeds springing out to find new ground,
put down new roots – something as simple
and complex as learning a new language, as life itself.

Journey to the Centre

1 Kata Tjuta

The invitation is to eternity – we follow the path
up the rocky slope between the opposing cliff faces
of the gorge. One is light and the other is dark,
both are pockmarked, water-streaked, rounded
and smoothed by millennia. In the shadow, the cliff face
and the ground take on a luminescence, an eerie red glow,
as if lit from within. We follow the crowd – French,
Japanese, American, Chinese…they have the assurance
of conquerors, occupying new land. The original inhabitants
are nowhere to be seen. But their presence is felt everywhere –
in the rocks that set the limits to the path, beyond which
we may not stray, in the tiny creek that trickles
down the gorge, between shallow pools – the only water
visible in a bone dry landscape – the vastness, the stillness,
and, in between the tourists, the silence of centuries.
We reach the viewing platform at the end of the path,
where a lone girl hiker sits amid the hubbub of clicking,
whirring cameras, chat, laughter, group poses and selfies,
ignoring it all, eyes closed, absorbing the peace, as it were,
through her skin. We shift location to the sunset viewing area,
where a quiet sunset warms the giant rocks to a gentle glow –
impressive enough, but hardly the spectacular light show
we were promised. We turn to go, but, as we do so, the sun
shoots out one last, parting flare, which ignites the rocks
in shades of brilliant orange and then, a golden flame.
It is exactly like looking into a fire, the rocks dissolving
into molten light, almost too bright to bear – but only
for a moment, before they sink back into night.
Nonetheless, we have been there, where we never
seriously expected to be – where rocks turn into flame,
movement to stillness, sound to silence, and time into eternity.

2 Uluru

A journey of the heart...I travel with my wife
and children to Uluru. I am wearing my bone fishhook –
hei matau – and thinking about my other family,
of whom there is only my younger brother left now...
from the heart of New Zealand to the heart of Australia.
We circumambulate the rock, complying with the request
of the local inhabitants that we refrain from climbing it,
angry at the other tourists, who brush right past the signs
asking them not to do so, in their eagerness to begin
the ascent. 'Let the monolith retain its mystery,' we think,
as we discover a world of different environments at its base,
from dry, sandy desert to densely bushed waterholes,
from giant geological features, which suggested stories
of the Dreamtime, to handprints and drawings of animals
in the cave galleries – humbler evidence of human occupation.
It is a matter of respect and disrespect, of knowledge
of what is appropriate and what is not appropriate,
like those subtle morals at the end of Dreamtime stories,
a deeper teaching, embodied in the place itself, to take
the time to sit, to breathe, to listen...to feel the peace
and hear the silence, which is not silence at all, but life
stirring in the leaves of the trees, in the birds, singing
on their branches, in the running water, in the blades of grass
rubbing softly together, in the loose, rolling grains of desert sand.

3 Leaving Uluru

While we wait in a stalled queue at the only
service station in town, my family and I watch
an Anangu family load jerrycans of petrol
into the back of their dusty, ageing station wagon,
preparing for a long journey to somewhere
that exists for them (the centre of their lives),
but nowhere that we can easily imagine.
How they differ from the rest of us – tourists,
grey nomads and truck drivers, who twitch
and fume at the delay and crowding – with
their barefoot nonchalance and ready laughter!
They are relaxed and at home, where we are
disoriented, on the edge of our awareness, lost,
one might almost say, in the desert. So it proves,
when, leaving town, we miss the turn-off to the airport
and start heading down the highway to Alice Springs.
Briefly, we experience that feeling of exhilaration,
that sense of infinite possibility at the start of a journey –
'Life is an open road and the sky's the limit!' – before
confusion closes in. Later, taking off from the airport,
I try for one last photo of Uluru over the plane's wing –
that massive lump of rock in the middle of the desert,
surrounded, as it seems to us, by empty space, a trackless
waste of red dust and olive scrub, a world of its own,
huge distances from anywhere else remotely recognisable
(except, perhaps, that artificial toytown of a resort nearby) –
a monument to time and timelessness, with its acolytes,
the skinny-trunked kurkaras, standing tall above the scrub,
all turning their scruffy heads towards the centre, ragged
band of devotees at a shrine we must shortly leave behind.

Two Days and Nights at Inverloch

1 Arrival

Swiping the keycard, we enter the room, with its view
of the ocean – white water breaking over the reef,
the Flat Rocks exposed by the falling tide like a dead man's bones.
There are kangaroos in the bottom paddock, down by the beach,
hopping gently about, bending over to feed, or standing stock-still,
tense with concentration, every sense attuned, balancing
on their thick, strong tails, before bending over to feed again.
The long, late afternoon light stretches from the old farmhouse
on the hill above, surrounded by its protective wall of trees,
past reef and rocks, the low, dark profile of the cape, with
its brilliantly shining wind farm, propellers whirling like soldiers
presenting arms on parade, down the inlet and away to the far hills.

2 Evening Walk

We walk through memory, past the caravan park
where we stayed with the children when they were small,
many years ago. It was here I took that photo of them,
confronting the strangeness of the sea. 'Not yet, O Lord, not yet!'
we prayed, later on, when they first felt ready to leave home.
The children may be grown up now and moved away,
finally launched on the great sea of life for themselves,
but the beach remains very much the same – the same
low dunes, covered with grass and scrub, and the same
miles of golden estuary sand, ribbed like an old man's wrinkled face
at low tide. The river cuts a sinuous blue line through it,
finding its way to the sea, flanked by stranded marker buoys,
like boats run aground, left high and dry, waiting for the tide
to float them again. We are reminded of the legendary sands of Dee.
How long, I wonder – as we retrace our line of footsteps, heading
back to shore – before the tide comes in, before we drown in memory?

3 Eagle's Nest

Driving along the narrow, winding coast road, we both gasp.
I pull the car over to the side of the road and we sit,
staring in disbelief, at two wings, frozen in stone, as if
a giant bird, spiralling down to its nest far below, had raised
its wings up in the last of flight, before folding them
along the sides of its body and settling there. We have to see more.
We park in the car park on the headland and walk down
steep wooden steps through thick bush on the side of the cliff,
across rock shelves on the beach with distinctive patterns –
cracked geometrically, like floor tiles, or lightly wrinkled,
like a crocodile's skin – out to the rock which is the eagle,
returning to its nest. Closer up, it resembles something else –
a cat, rising in alarm, ears pricked, tail high, eyes glaring.
Closer still, it is what it is – a massive lump of rock,
carved with intricate evidence of weathering. Its sheer size
is overwhelming, let alone thought of its age and origins.
What gigantic forces separated it from the rest of the cliff
or pushed it up through the seabed? What endless, patient action
of wind and water shaped that illusion of landing bird or rising cat?
What paradoxical genius of nature made heavy stone so light
that it could fly – or so it seemed – as freely as imagination?

4 Bunurong People

We walk to the top of the hill, behind the resort.
From here, the view is enormous: ocean, inlet, cape
(with a glimpse of the distant, triple-humped Prom
surfacing over its shoulder, like a promise of paradise,
where everything is unspoiled – nature in a state
of primal innocence). The sky arches over all, its vast dome
a stainless, indifferent blue on this cloudless day.
The original inhabitants, the Bunurong, would gather here
before following the creek down to the swamp
at the bottom of the hill where they would feast on roots,
berries, waterfowl, fish and – presumably – kangaroos.
We follow them down in our turn, temporary visitors
and instant experts, thanks to information provided
on welcome benches, placed conveniently along the way.
The Bunurong would also conduct initiations at the swamp,
taking the inexperienced young and making them
familiar with their way of life on the surrounding land –
with one exception, apparently. That promontory was just
too pure, too pristine to be seen by those not properly prepared.
They had to view it through a screen of leaves, as if perfection
were too confronting, too difficult for untrained sight to stand.
The Bunurong are gone now, cleared away to another location
down the coast, leaving this evidence of their dispossession,
this sad, earnest, belated attempt to pay respect to their loss.

5 Dinosaurs

On one side of the corridor between reception and our room,
a glass case containing fossilized dinosaur remains
draws our attention. There is a claw – the first fossil
found in the area, says the accompanying text – some tiny teeth,
proving, the text continues, not all creatures of that era were huge,
and a larger thigh bone ('That's more like it!' we exclaim, ever
eager to be impressed). They are all reminders, the text concludes,
of the time when Australia was still joined to Antarctica
and this selection of prehistoric animals (and others like them)
survived – indeed, thrived – in the glacial chill one hundred
and twenty million years ago. We drive to the Caves, where
such remains are found – another stretch of rock-shelved beach
at the foot of cliffs, like so much of the coast round here. We walk
out to the low tide line, where generations of university students
have shovelled sand from rock pools to uncover fossil-bearing rocks.
Playing palaeontologists, we search for likely rocks ourselves,
but can, of course, find none. Tiring of our fruitless game, we wander
round the headland to check the caves that give the place its name.
Menaced by a roaring tide, we peek into entrances, but do not dare go in.
Curiously female, the caves hint at damp, dark mysteries they contain.
They bring back the miracle of origin, the place where the world began.

6 Departure

We return to the present. On departure day, the carpark
is full for the first time. Some conference or convention
is in occupation. Voices, music, the sounds of a PA
and smell of breakfast barbecue filter through the trees.
We hand in our keycards, pay our bill, then take the highway
back to the city. By the Phillip Island turnoff, the traffic
is thickening. By Cranbourne, it has curdled like cream.
We crawl along the freeway towards a city dominated
by the spires of cranes, symbols of the new religion
of over-development. It's everybody's party but ours,
it seems – specially the developers'. Apartment blocks
rise like cakes with brightly coloured icing, or towering,
phallic candles in the civic heartland, causing yet more
traffic delays. This is not a future we ever dreamed of
or wanted. We stand outside it, like passengers, stranded
on a platform, watching the train leave the station
without us, heading for an unknown destination, while we –
old fossils, empty-nesters that we are – make our slow way home.

Waiting at the Sydenham Rail Crossing

The alarm bell rings, the warning lights flash,
the boomgate jerks down, the traffic grinds to a halt.
Twenty-five years of waiting in this spot –
the rail crossing at Sydenham! Nothing to do
but sit behind the wheel, silently stewing, eyeing
the clock, waiting for the 8.20 from Bendigo to pass
and its companion, the 8.22 from Southern Cross,
to pass the other way. The old Sydenham railway station
is boarded up, graffitied, abandoned, replaced
by a gleaming glass and steel box and a steel footbridge
over the tracks where pedestrians used to play
Russian roulette with the trains. Twenty-five years
of waiting in this spot while the empty paddocks
changed to a massive shopping strip and housing estate –
black-roofed Macmansions as far as the eye can see!
I used to joke this was the end of the earth, the exact
mid-point of nowhere, crossing into outer darkness.
Now it is simply the start of another suburb.
I sit and wait. I think of all the cars I have waited in
here – my own and others, by myself or car-pooling,
the blare of the radio, the incessant chat of teachers,
friendships made and broken – and now, here I am,
on my own again. Twenty-five years of teaching
in the west, twenty-five years of educating
the sons and daughters of the working class (who may
or may not have appreciated the opportunity)
and I am still here, waiting for the trains to pass!
Is this where my life went? Nothing is as transient
as stillness. Soon the bells will stop ringing, the lights
will no longer flash, the boomgate will jerk upwards
and the traffic will move on. The suburb will continue
to grow, with or without me. I wait for the signal to go.

Lunch at Noodleland

In memory of Jim Fawns, educational psychologist

Oh, those lunches at Noodleland! – tom yum for you,
laksa for me, curry puffs and nasi goreng for Daniel,
watching the waggers sneak through the parking lot
outside the window…or a bottle of red after work
on a Friday night – your favourite, Gramp's Grenache,
with Blau Castello or anchovies, straight from the jar,
while the wit (and the gossip) flowed up and down the table,
the sounds of people who worked a hard job relaxing,
letting go, easing themselves into the weekend…
and no one worked harder than you at a more difficult,
thankless task, propping up young lives that had already
gone seriously astray – teenagers, pregnant, out of home,
abused, betrayed by those they should have had most
trust in, bullied, depressed, unable to read or write…
they all came to your door, broken lives, waiting to be fixed,
to be put back together, pointed on a new path, which
you gladly accepted as your task, your responsibility,
the boundaries defined only by the size of your heart.
'This is a shit place!' the kids cried, their voices filled
with anguish, rage or hate, the harsh, echoing sound
of a community at odds with itself, while you listened,
calmed them, brought them hope – more than that,
gave them a plan, some way out… 'I love these kids!'
you would say, often the only one who did (and how you
would have hated to hear me say this – you, who never
worked for reputation or for gain!). I sometimes wonder
if your heart was too big, or not big enough. Whichever,

in the end, it wore out. Ah, Jim, wherever you are listening
to a young person in trouble, sitting down to a good steak,
teeing off, putting a bet on, or following your beloved Bombers,
I lift my glass of red, my spoonful of laksa, one more time to you…

The Last Yard Duty

A lone adult islanded in a sea of adolescents,
I stand outside the school on Monday morning yard duty,
watching the tide of students roll in. No one walks
or rides any more. They are all delivered by their parents –
an endless succession of cars, utes, trucks
and 4-wheel drives, pulling up to the kerb – wave after wave
breaking on the school shore. Students spring out
of seats, bags are retrieved, doors slammed, goodbyes called.
They stop being sons and daughters and become
their other selves, the performance they reserve for their peers.
Friends are greeted, extravagant hugs exchanged,
which go to show 'I am not alone; I am known here; I belong.'
They chat enthusiastically about the trivia
of yesterday, as if they have been away for years, voyaging,
and not just overnight. Slowly, they pair off
and drift inside like lazy tongues of water, running up sand.
The bell tolls, or beeps. I chase the remnants along,
leaving only the most lonely ones, tenaciously lingering on,
in anticipation of that special friend, who
will not come today. Then they, too, drift off, disappointed.
The sea is calmed for another morning; the last wave
has broken. Time to resume my teaching duties, an old man
who has been here longer than anyone can remember,
part of the school, like the gum-encrusted, grafittied furniture –
a grey, weathered piece of driftwood, cast up
on that shore – backdrop to their dramas, about whom
they hardly care. They are coming; I am going;
there is always young life, new hope, everywhere.

Freedom

'A holiday, a holiday, the first one of the year…' – 'Little Matty Grove'
                'O victory
forget your underwear we're free' – Allen Ginsberg, *Howl*

I'm driving along Rathdowne Street, past the Commission flats and the Carlton pool, towards Rathdowne Village. The leaves of the pin oaks are green against the blue sky. It's a perfect day of early autumn – the best time of year in Melbourne. I've got the windows rolled down for the heat; traffic noise fills my ears. There's a singing rising inside me. It's like the last day of term, driving out the school gates, heading down the long highway home. The road is clear before me, like the empty days, waiting to be filled with the pleasures of freedom…nothing can hold me back, unless it be the inevitable return up that same highway, which I know I must eventually make. The thought almost clouds my day. Then I remember – there's no return this time. I'm retired now. For once in my life, I'm truly free. Suddenly, fear strikes…what will I do with this freedom? Or rather, what will it do with me? What freedom do I have – the freedom to do or to be? And can there be freedom without limits? Somehow it seems I'm always running into them – either the inevitable return, or, at the end of it all, the point of no return, which seems even worse. These thoughts are like a dark shadow, passing under the trees. Then on into light again, which flickers on bonnet and windscreen, at forty kilometres an hour, down my favourite street – not so much full speed ahead as slow motion behind the other traffic – free of doubt, free of fear, the blood singing in my ears now, chanting 'Freedom, freedom, freedom!' It doesn't matter, really, to or from what…the only thing that matters is I'm finally free!

Mendelssohn Octet

They came from right across middle-class Melbourne,
old, white-haired, firm and infirm, with a smattering
of the young among them – those last, surviving lovers
of classical music. They came to the ark auditorium,
with its worm-riddled timber panelling, like the hull
of an old sailing ship, and its giant chandeliers,
like upside down jellyfish, floating above them.
They came to sit in comfortable, cushioned rows,
chattering warmly with each other, until the lights dimmed,
the musicians filed in, silence fell (apart from the odd,
hesitant cough) and the music began, stealing over them
like a dream. Brahms, something modern (but not
too modern), then – after the interval – the Mendelssohn.
The musicians were standing now, as if there were
too much energy in this music to sit down –
the irrepressible energy of a teenager, discovering
his indisputable genius at sixteen – winding
the broad river of his melody through the first movement,
raising the spectre of ethereal beauty in the second,
like the brush of an an angel's wing, and on to the finish,
the instruments weaving around each other
with ever-growing confidence, complexity and speed,
in a dance of sheer joy, ending with a triumphant blaze
of sound. The air felt charged with energy afterwards,
as the audience leapt (metaphorically) to applaud –
not exactly on their feet, but very enthusiastically,
from the plush security of their seats. 'Beauty is born,'
the music said, 'it lives, it can transform your lives.'
and they seemed grateful, those good bourgeois,
as they shuffled out into the light of a mundane
Melbourne afternoon. They had been touched by a flame;
their lives, young and old, would never be quite the same.

'The Seasons' With Vincent Van Gogh, at the NGV

Impossible not to wonder what Vincent
would have made of such a queue, snaking
up and down the Great Hall many times,
before finally entering the exhibition space.
The artist as celebrity – an indisputable art star –
not the grumpy drunk that Jeanne Calment
remembered from her uncle's store in Arles,
unsuccessful and increasingly isolated,
subject to repeated hospitalisation. Enough
to make you weep, if it weren't so beautiful –
the long journey into light, from dank winter
in the north to the full blaze of summer
in the south…and beyond. Beware of getting
what you wish for, as the old saying has it,
or why must what we most want always
destroy us, whether it be God, light, heat,
or all three? Because life keeps on proliferating,
like the tendrils of the vine, snaking out of control,
or the luxurious spring growth in the asylum garden,
a riot of colour and shape. It won't stop,
like the thoughts that multiply inside a brain,
the constant struggle between hope and despair,
leading…where? Not to the stone bench,
which waits so invitingly in the shade,
seeming to say, 'I'm tired. I want to rest.'
It keeps right on, past the point of vision fulfilled,
mastery attained over an exacting medium

among the blazing fields, to where the Mistral blows,
stirring the grass, twisting the cypresses, cutting
the clouds into strange, menacing shapes, turning
the sky pale, poisonous green, the heat and light
consuming everything…or that final self-portrait,
with one, wild eye that stares out at the spectator,
attacking, devouring the world, while the other eye
turns inward, retiring, reflective, too gentle
and too sensitive to stand living for much longer,
and the whole covered in a flurry of brushstrokes,
as if to say 'More colour, more contrast yet!
There's never enough…' Light tones on a dark ground,
dark on a light, faster and faster, until everything
begins to spin – coloured dashes, evidence
of where one hand has been, recorded
now and forever, radiating out to infinity…

Of Hoons and Balloons

Driving down the freeway outside Traralgon,
an ageing, white HSV rockets past me, full
of yahooing teenage males, complete
with T-shirts, tatts and backwards caps.
'Hoons!' I sniff, all righteous, middle-aged
indignation. 'They'll either kill themselves
or somebody else, or both.' A paper bag
from some fast food franchise, thrown
carelessly out their window, rises and falls
like a parachute in their wake.
                      Speeding and littering! –
My heart cries out against them, doubly
appalled. Then I look again and see it is
no paper bag, but a pinky-red balloon,
borne by those currents they leave behind them
in their headlong rush along the road. I almost
laugh with relief at the unexpected beauty of it,
the trivial joy it brings. The car itself is rapidly
lost to sight ahead, but more and more balloons
came floating back, red, green, blue, yellow
and white, a surreal cloud of childish delight.
Phallic or breast-like (sausage dog or plump
full moon?), they nose the roadside grasses,
or bounce higher than the treetops, happy in
the artificial breeze. There is something
touching in their fragility – contrasted with our
brute machines – and their delicate pastel shades,
opposed to the highway's monochrome grey.

They bring life and laughter with them, where
previously I was thinking only of destinations,
of 'being there', the journey over, as quickly,
safely and painlessly as possible, a clean,
anaesthetised going. And so I bless them,
as I curse them, those highway hoons, for
the shock of feeling that my life was threatened,
but having brought some joy into it, too.

On Finding a Jehovah's Witness Magazine Jammed in the Door of Our Country Home

The attention is flattering, but why would someone
walk all the way from our closed front gate to the house,
which is obviously unoccupied, in order to bring us
the good news that Jesus loves us and, out of the millions
of – I am sure – more deserving souls, wants to save us?
Thus, it is that, arriving at our country property, we find
a copy of *The Watchtower* thrust into our front door
for the first time I have seen it since the Brooklyn shore
(of which the JWs own a fair chunk), waving forlornly
in the breeze, as if to say, 'Hey, out there, remember me?
There is still a dim possibility that you might repent
your wicked ways and join the elite, the beloved of God,
when the last trumpet sounds.' The opportunity for love
hangs before us, like the last leaf on an autumn tree.
Tear it out, summarily, and consign it to its unconsidered fate
in the rubbish bin! Once, millions would have died for such
a prospect, such a faith. Now we deride the lonely, deluded soul
who trudged all that way just to bring us the unwanted news.

Night Piece

I wake in the middle of the night and look out between curtains, open for the heat, at the sky, descending on the house at the top of the hill across the road. Heavily pendulous, the errant constellations tumble down the sky towards the house, brilliantly lit, from far off, by porch lights and flickering plasma TV. Like Prometheus bringing fire to humans, the house seems to conduct the brilliance of the night sky to earth, but only in limited portion. The hill itself is dark, like this room where I lie, in the house of the dying man, sweating, unable to sleep.

Halfway and Back

i.m. Roger Brundle (1946–2016)

You were paler than the sheets on which you lay –
almost translucent – and painfully thin, except for
the swelling mound in the centre of your body.
Delicate as a girl, you talked in a whisper, returned
to the hospital you hated with a chest infection –
more proof, if it was needed, of the disease ravaging
your body, opening it to the menaces of every passing bug.
But that didn't stop you from your reminiscences
about driving round Australia in your Land Rover
with the off-road caravan on the back.

                                                Your voice grew stronger,
as you explained to your layman audience technicalities
of the caravan's suspension, and stronger still, talking
about time spent in Broome, where you watched the moon,
one spring night, cast its eerie, beautiful, silver ladder
across the sea and pools of water on the sand. Thoroughly
warmed up now, you told a funny story about a barmaid
at the Cameron's Corner pub. When you asked her
for an ashtray, she replied – exquisite as her surroundings –
'What's wrong with the fuckin' floor?' You roared
with laughter, as best you could (ending with a fit of coughing),
and we roared with you.

      Then Fay talked about staying
at Uluru, her voice tinged with awe as she described
the overpowering size and beauty of the rock, viewed
from its base, and how much she wanted to walk around it
with you and the guide, but felt too tired. She perked up,
however, when the guide suggested, 'Why not walk
halfway and back?' 'OK,' she said, falling for the guide's
age-old trap. 'Then I thought,' she continued, 'I might as well
go the whole way.' So she did. We all laughed again,
then sat in silence, thinking about that red rock, rising
from the middle of that vast, red earth desert – a long,
lingering silence, a single heartbeat filling the room.

Entering the Crematorium

Entering the crematorium, the young boy stops
on the entrance mat. He scissors his legs,
spins around, puts his right foot out, pulls it in,
puts his left foot out, pulls it in and waves
his arms in the air. He has truly arrived at the house
of death where his grandfather lies. This is not
to say he celebrates his grandfather's death, but rather
his own young life – after sitting all afternoon,
listening to grown ups talk about a man he hardly knew,
he finally has a chance to move. So he takes it.
Young life dances at the door of death, as it always does –
and has a right to do – the past is just a rumour,
the future is so far away and only the present is here.

Return to Castlemaine

Death is impossible to write about, it has been said,
except as a gap, an absence, like a missing tooth
or a hole in the ground. That's what it comes down to –
a hole in the ground – or rather, a plaque on the side
of a rose bed, overlooking the bowl of the cemetery,
nestled between trees below. It seems a fitting place
to make an end, like a gallery seat with a theatre view –
a theatre of the dead, where all are buried so they face
the rising sun (as the cemetery caretaker tells us),
except these annoying few up on the hill. But this is
no cause for argument; there is a deep, abiding peace
in this bush setting, between earth and wind and leaves.
A man might well never move again, surrounded by
such peace. Life is difficult and painful, a precious
opportunity which can be surprisingly easy to waste,
but, after its turbulence, its boredom, its petty resentments
and its great, enduring loves, it seems appropriate that
a man should come to rest here, on the side of a hill,
beneath the trees, above the cemetery, with its carefully
regulated rows, absorbing the warmth of the afternoon sun.

Night of the Supermoon

The time is out of joint, as Prince Hamlet said,
and I certainly wasn't born to set it right.
A con-man and bully becomes President. The whole
world trembles in anticipation. An old poet dies.
That part of the world (much smaller) which is still
literate and compassionate mourns. The poet set it
to music years ago. 'Sail on, oh mighty ship of state…'
he intoned, ironically, against a background
of rattling snare drums . We will need his irony
in the years to come. And yet, and yet…I can still
walk out my front door at two o'clock in the morning,
my iPhone in my hand, and photograph the moon,
which glows above me like the biggest, brightest spotlight
you've ever seen, a witness to love and truth, if not
to justice. No paternal ghost stalks the battlements tonight,
but the injunction remains: not revenge but reversal,
while we can, restoration of the right, however (and by whomever)
that is to be achieved – preferably, without the tragedy.

Space Station Passing Over Our House in West Preston, 11.1.17

Tipped off by our space photographer nephew,
we stand out on our suburban street
at a quarter to ten at night to see the space station
cross the enormous sky above our tiny
corner of the world. With our binoculars, we search
the sky, desperate for a glimpse. First,
we think it might be Venus, shining brightly above
the dark pines of the cemetery at the end
of the street – love triumphing over death, after all…
Suddenly, we see it, a travelling light, high up
in the dome of the sky, moving with surprising speed
and certainty along its preordained path
towards its goal – the far-distant horizon – where
it vanishes from sight. It orbits the earth
once every ninety minutes, they say, nimbly threading
its way between asteroids and satellites –
the general litter of space debris – a fragile container
of hope, symbol of faith in a united, off-world,
high-tech future, while we turn and walk slowly back
to our house in the divided, declining world below.

The Lumber Room

'A room where disused and bulky things are kept' – *Oxford Dictionaries*
'A room for storing old pieces of furniture and things that are not being used' – *Merriam-Webster Dictionary*

The 'lumber room', as they used to call it.
in those English children's novels, set
in grand old houses – we have one
at the front of our house (though we are
anything but grand – quite the reverse).
It was a room children found on a rainy day,
gingerly removing the dust sheets, promising
magic, a journey back in time, adventures
with the ancestors. Our ancestors are all
well and truly dead, and likely to remain so:
nonetheless, we keep our past in that room
at the front of our house, stuffed to the gills
with old furniture, the 'lumber' from
our holiday house in the country, now sold,
plus whatever our children left behind
when they moved out of home – the detritus
of thirty years. 'Disused and bulky' is right;
they fill the room at odd angles, like pieces
of a jigsaw that don't really fit together,
or people elbowing each other on a crowded bus.
The past is a river we swim in like fish, or cyclists,
threading their way through rush-hour traffic.
carefully avoiding obstacles, entanglements,
and even outright danger – boxes piled high
on other boxes, pictures stacked haphazardly
on table tops, a fridge with its doors gaping open,

wire hangers dangling off portable clothes racks,
jiggling ominously in the faintest breath of air,
standing lamps leaning at precarious angles,
bedside tables dumped upside down on armchairs.
bookshelves crammed to overflowing, bedding
spilled across an ageing couch…

       Every morning,
I pick my way along the narrow path between
the layers to open the blinds and shed some light
on the chaotic scene. That done, I retire, closing
the door behind me lest our family secrets be exposed.
The past is not something we live with easily, rather
it calls for private inspection, private reflection –
sometimes a cause of pride, sometimes of shame,
definitely not for public consumption. Really,
it's an encumbrance, something we can't bring
ourselves to part with, slowly gathering dust
in a closed room, a ghostly reminder of who
we were and where we've been…in our generation,
let alone those who came before.

      So, I come back to myself,
as I step outside that room, into the clear light
of the hall, mercifully empty of everything
except the everyday items that we use now.
The past will bury us – it threatens to overwhelm us
like a breaking wave, if we don't leave it behind;

it will grind our faces in the sand and leave us
waterlogged, choking in its wake. When will
life end? When it's all past, like that wave,
running on up the beach, and that moment will come
too soon, if we can't bring ourselves to say
goodbye to what, apparently, has such a hold on us:
our own pasts, good and bad, the everlasting recital,
the never ending balancing act, heading towards
the final summation, coupled with – buffered by –
faded imaginings of grander times and circumstances.
the magic and adventure of the 'lumber room',
the rainy day children discovering the ancestors
under dust sheets, everything that was promised
by those old children's novels, now gathering dust
themselves, in that room at the front of our house.

Towards Dawn

Towards dawn, I turn to you and lay
my arm along your marble thigh,
as smooth and firm as any schoolgirl's
still, or wrap it round your softer belly,
which has borne two children, now
grown up. It's true I'm no good at
simple affection – I always want to take it
further – but I wouldn't dare to wake you, so
I cling to your semi-naked warmth, instead,
like a child would cling to its mother,
waking in the night, in our island bed,
in the middle of our room, as the chilly light
penetrates the blinds and the early birds
begin to sing their beautiful, intricate melodies.

Reasons Not to Leave Home

(Once again) for Joy

There are many places in this world
worth travelling to (and many, many
more we will never know about),
but sometimes it's better to stay home.
There is the Virginia creeper spreading itself
across the front fence like a green stain,
slowly flushing heart's blood red; there are
the maple trees, waving fresh, young fingers
of goodbye, which dry, over time, to wrinkled,
leathery bronze; then there is the jasmine,
sweetly scenting the entry, like a mother's embrace
in childhood, on returning home; and the…
but you know what I mean. There are so many
uncompleted projects vying for attention
out in the back garden: the shed stands,
half-stripped of paint, like an underwear-clad
actress from a French farce, waiting
in the wings for her cue; the circular bed
cries out for weeding like a baby's mouth –
that O of unassuageable, repeated need;
the fruit trees' boughs bend under the weight
of unpicked fruit and threaten to break,
if we don't relieve them of their burden –
their precious, much-anticipated crop
becoming food, once again, for the birds.

Nonetheless, it's out the back that
we like to sit, commanding the garden
from the heights of the porch, like generals,
planning our next campaign; or out
on the lawn, in the full blaze of the sun,
lying back on recliners, like Hollywood stars
beside the pool; or at the far end of the garden,
sipping iced drinks like Connecticut housewives
on Cape Cod chairs in the dappled shade –
a tented coolness, like the sudden cold patch,
discovered, diving to the bottom, in the shallows
of a summer sea – a place to rest when
we are tired after a busy day, a busy life…
half a lifetime (at least) of work and family,
like a route march with heavy packs
through unfamiliar territory, a journey
with unreliable maps to an uncertain destination,
but enormously relieved to have arrived, at last.
All these constitute reasons not to leave,
to cleave, instead, to this life we have made
for ourselves here, in this place, this time –
this fundamental rightness, finally.

Acknowledgements

'Walking With My Dog By the Merri Creek' was published in *Inscribe*, Winter Edition, 2012.

'Waiting at the Sydenham Rail Crossing' won the Poetica Christi Prize, 2013.

'Driving to the Supermarket' was published in *A Lightness of Being*, Poetica Christi Press, 2014.

An earlier, slightly different, version of 'Farewell to Kendrick and Mary' was commended in the Woorilla Poetry prize, 2015.

'Halfway and Back' won the Glen Phillips Poetry Prize, 2016.

'The Lumber Room' was highly commended in the June Shenfield Poetry Award, 2016.

'Night Piece' was published in *Grieve*, Hunter Writers Centre, 2016.

'1976' was highly commended in the Adelaide Plains Poetry Competition, 2017.

'Space Station Passing Over Our House in West Preston' was published in *Ear to Earth*, Central Coast Poets Inc., 2017.

Parts of 'On the Death of Neil Armstrong' were used in the video *In Memory of Neil Armstrong* and the whole poem was published in the catalogue for the *Apollo 11*, a video homage to the moon landing event touring exhibition, 2019.

About the Author

Stephen Smithyman is a retired schoolteacher who lives in Melbourne. His poems have appeared in a range of publications such as *Rabbit, Australian Poetry Journal, Cordite* and the *Poetry New Zealand Yearbook*. He won the Victorian Cancer Council Outstanding Poem award, 2011, Poetica Christi prize, 2013, and the Glen Phillips Poetry Prize, 2016. A collection of poems, *Snapshot in the Dark*, was published by Ginninderra Press in 2018.

www.ingramcontent.com/pod-product-compliance
Lightning Source LLC
Chambersburg PA
CBHW062149100526
44589CB00014B/1751